Sky Ward

Wesleyan Poetry

Sky Ward

Kazim ali

Wesleyan University Press
Middletown, Connecticut

Wesleyan University Press

Middletown CT 06459

www.wesleyan.edu/wespress

© 2013 Mohammad Kazim Ali

All rights reserved

Manufactured in the United States of America

Designed and typeset in Seria Sans by Eric M. Brooks

Wesleyan University Press is a member of the
Green Press Initiative. The paper used in this book
meets their minimum requirement for recycled paper.

ART WORKS.
arts.gov

This project is supported in part by a grant from
the National Endowment for the Arts.

Library of Congress Cataloging-in-Publication Data

Ali, Kazim, 1971–

Sky ward / Kazim Ali. — 1st ed.

    p. cm. — (Wesleyan poetry)

Poems.

ISBN 978-0-8195-7357-5 (cloth: alk. paper) —

ISBN 978-0-8195-7358-2 (ebook)

I. Title.

PS3601.L375S55   2013

811'.6 — dc23   2012030229

5 4 3 2 1

Contents

Sky Ward

Follower

Hollow the ear in its lathe dark urge to bind in afterlife
      the temporal word
When the white-leafed arms flew up in prayer I left

Father, will the sun always unwing me?
How else will I

1

Journey to Providence

body a window is thrown is throne
sewn along the seam of I

courage an empty bowl drained or teeming
drowned or sown along what seems like sky

well came the problem of where to live
driving through the gray evening, cold rain on the windows
listening to melancholy piano on the radio

why can't I look at people when I am speaking to them
my touch is an argument for pleasure or pressure
mornings I run whipstill and drunk at the body's rage

gorgeous I miss
not salvation but bliss I adore
discs of green melting snow reveals

When the journal of music gave way
to the journal of pain the pages curled
themselves into fists and wept

but will I broken will I undone
at the water ask to go deeper a boat
dusting linden clears away envy

wandering like lilac snow in dunes
never the water enter the duskwarm room
will I let you wing me will I have leapt skyward

there is a dream past all unsleeping
a fire turned friend and held
if we are wedded how does the wind go through me

carving monoliths and caves
valley conversant in streaks of light
my tongue disappear into dusk's many tongues

there is no one to write this sadness how hard it is
going to be to live without him a lonely gathering
a haze a crated shrine air thick and healing itself

unraveled collapsed into who would have known
the cost of breaking I could have told you
with a lurch we are all of a sudden airborne

prepare to open the leaves not a canticle of wind but reverie
      or revelation
the black square perhaps meaning a dissolving of the body into
      the ground
though isn't this what you were promised and crave

here on the frightened bluff naked in the moonlight
with a view of the foundry spitting up flames and liquid stone
everything we love has been lost we are in a wilderness

you will get told bell astral buoy hurricane eye
night soaking the foothills in lambent downpour
a storm front approaching with the gentlest touch

never care atlas let the cold in from every corner
something has recessed you have noticed this before of course
the rain has not yet fallen but still fiery felt on the skin

why say out the beach's syllables dark recess you climbed
dare you say salvation what can it mean to the unmoment saved
it works to fold into a thousand flying cranes

one moment we came to an empty house in the country
          and wondered
who lived there the next moment we were a wild boat refusing
to return to harbor even at the storm's violent height

glass you remember the other life:
rain, the beach, his breath hot on your neck
what are we if not lost in pools of blame

sunlight yield the harshest corner
where the last words still stray
what you want most is to hold breath in you

Lake House

Now to praise utterly unceasing
now to shadow and learn

Flickering pulse   last chapter sent
Never to touch   be shorn

Full hour spent spelling my house
by web to thread air blue

By cover of night tree to tree
strung any place through

Seen clear sun   cold lake soul
found any place home

Now done under   woven to spill

Blue night lake foal

Divination

Your son turns restive in his sleep
Whispered away by morning to dusk

Verses bloom along his wrists and throat
In bright sentences his name is cut

Five times a day he cries out
His voice snuffed in flowery wells

He knows in his heart none can take you truly in
Save the house that unhomed you

Fairy Tale

In the acres of garden before an empty house an amnesiac prince collects broken branches, prunes the fruit trees, plucks weeds from the rock bed.

He speaks a broken language of beach and Broadway and on the way to shore gets lost and finds himself in a cemetery at sunset, pink light on the stones.

He cannot read the inscriptions but kneels down at a cenotaph anyhow and recites the only prayers he can remember.

Why, when we wanted to speak to nothing but water, is he singing verses down into the stone hard earth in a town he has never belonged to, lost on his way to the shore?

If only he would learn to read the book of the sky, he would see the birds circling lazily around hot currents, which could only mean a large body of water is near.

The words are hollow in his mouth and he doesn't know what he believes anyhow, whether bodies will again rise or if the aerial rumors of the gulls will lead him to the sea or if the numb tombstone in his mouth might indeed speak.

His scripture comes out sideways and his mispronunciation of the most sacred of syllables makes him always friendless. It's nearly a party trick the way he opens his mouth and butterflies pour out, closes it again and the clock chimes, reminding him of being a young boy, coming home to an empty house, sure that he had been forgotten, that everyone had gone to the beach without him.

Sure that he would always be forgotten, that he would lie down in his grave and no ghost would come to fetch him or explain god or what was supposed to happen next.

That the grave would fill with dirt and he would rise on the boat of his body. That no one would recite sacred chapters for him, that he wouldn't know how to take the rudder, that the sea was too far.

The boat now coming apart, his voice dwindling, hard as stone.

Finally he sees a bird winging down calling, "Find-me, find-me!"

But he doesn't understand words, only sound, the shape of words, the tune to which they are sung.

All the sacred verses in the world are like birds wheeling in the sky, who knows where they go.

High Stakes Game

Little by little I strife I come by
holding dark felt aloft

Outsmarting winter's final blue scene
I see the outline of invisible water

See me winter
Raise me felt and snow

Freeze Tag

Why agree to this awful treaty

To share the fate of fire and flesh

Released from stillness by a single touch

For barely one moment being able to think "I"

Through stone or muck we run as if on fire

Fingers reaching to save all the others

No return home but an eternity of transformation

Everyone crying out   not-it   not-it

Baptism

Ashamed and almost withering
when the winged god flew from my throat

I wanted to kill him for wanting him
begged to be reborn as a brute or beast but

it was me who wanted to be killed like a king,
my uncertain body chained to the rocks promising

to lie still, to be destroyed, wanting only
to kiss the hands of my winged assassin

I would break any promise to be so
daily devoured, eternally delivered —

Frozen

Daily I wish stitched here to live

Facing west watching the last light

Tattooed on my left wrist, "let-go"

Tattooed on my right wrist, "not-it"

Daily you make me dizzy with messages

Nightly torn open by brute sky and eagle claw

The strongest man in the world is on his way to release me

But what happens when a frozen man is touched by fire

Upon release I may disappear

The Nowhere House

chrysalis drinking brought me brought me certain and dour

shadow intoxicant lust me

brahmacharya charlatan commit your crime

saint olga broumas seize me
saint shahid ali sees me

still as that starving humble boy who stumbled
north up the river from the city thrusting

every time I look into the house of nowhere
sound hums under

weigh me down and need me
saint sufi anyone knead me

Prayer Request Cards

I would like the church to pray for

    a clear reckoning
    the core unearthed
    what's best born skyward
    searched

    who's most easily followed
    seared

    who's most faithful
    beckoned to
    queer

I would like the church to pray

    my psalm to unsettle the case
    my askance umbilical lust to review
    and refute the evidence

    to enter my gilt-edged tongue
    as final proof
    of innocence

I would like the church

    on the inside of my sin
    to spell out my breath
    to draw a wing

The Good Brother

A penniless pot-maker I am always willing to condemn or be
sentenced.

Oh yes, as the fan turned in the hot afternoon I bore witness to
the sadness of our father, working his way through blade and stone,
hungry to guide his son.

I am the good brother, never to know more, never to look at the
far shore.

For a decade I made pilgrimage to the river, scoping out the place
I heard my brother fell.

Brother of the bird, I watched from a distance wondering if I would
have had the courage to listen to our father.

Still unbelieving, I remain in the lair of the beast; only half a man,
I declined the coat my brother wore, incandescent aspect of both bird
and angel.

Ticket

I dug graves in my pockets searching for the ticket out.
Intent on escape I never noticed there was no wall.

I lash myself daily describing fake bondage:
All the prisons and pockets, the graves in which I bury myself.

Swoon

small sound pocket
sky torn wound

down my body
eight limbed swoon

lunar starved catastrophe
across the midline stranded

stranger street lantern
leading to winter

time unwrought sore
still who are you

no where ecstatic
beside yourself now

Crib

to you I seed myself a crib of roots
tide in and out sail me ashore

wide eye wild year other side of fall
forests close tight your hands

wild spring never leave me
tide out my bonecase my ever

I am harridan-mad and sore
every body I love is dying

Bright Felon Deleted Scene 3

Amelia looking at photographs of my vacation says, "There are no people in them!"

There are only mountains, clouds, empty streets, two pictures of my back.

Uncontained in silence the sun is eclipsed.

In Dante's Hell, him with my name is split neck to navel and stuffed with maggots and grubs.

"You're turning your back on people," says Amelia.

But on the subway I steal glances at your ear, your cheek, your chin, when I think you are not looking.

It's not true, it's not true. Your mouth, your hand, your ankle, your thigh.

I am an inferno of fallen creatures, all wriggling for the light.

Launch

Unmake yourself year by year
Your urge surges in your ear

No purpose at all but dispersal
tools of everywhere time

strange cup spilled the gap of fill
no one your brethren seem

no bestial stranger disturbing your house
no odd shattered flowering bed

a hagiography of feathers glued
to your sin-singed skin

aim for the sun, singing
in long unforgotten tongues

I'm leaving you behind
A ghost of a prayer

Leaving you behind
a shining thread

2

Twin

I've never stopped looking for my twin in the rain,
not him but me who is the long-lost brother.

He is safe in our mountain home remembering nothing
of the wound inside, the emptiness that lingers.

The rocky trail leading to the shrine of my name-saint,
collapsed in pieces, alarmed by the rattling sibilance.

Loneliness my enemy, risky and intentional,
a single line of pilgrims interrupted by abstraction.

How can we speak of ordinary things when my blank chapter
is still out there somewhere unaware and unwritten

Shrine

Suppliant I lost myself
soul moment to stone
raised myself to disappear

Sky is not I
sent down and endless
Nowhere emerging

No cenotaph shimmering with kisses
in the room of my interrupted life
no name saint anywhere anymore

Autobiography

begin at the earliest hour
     is there a self

at the corner of San Anton and Duende I hardly know
the edge of the sidewalk a bare consonant
of the city's harsh sentence

how can I say my actual name
when all I can manage is counting change
for coffee I do not buy

every night the clouds argue in the sky
for the right to be the one who will part
to reveal the new moon

blank but appearing
day by day
a new misunderstanding of gone

how can you already know if you have never yet been
the twin inside arriving after departure
the crime of history a quivering vessel

my also bones a manic making
who am I a man inside a bell inside someone else's face
fingers that hold a skull or pen

of course a swan could be an elephant or a man could be on fire
the coffee I didn't drink is pouring through time
inside any city a thousand vowels pronounce themselves

every street map has a thousand
pointing arrows labeled
"You are here"

but who are you
at the corner of San Anton and Duende
dark-eyed and holding your empty

no body knows you
hardly arriving and
already gone

The Escape

Father whose purpose swims
while the universe mends itself

Wind was water
porpoise was prophet

Father my swim
the sutured eventual blue splinters

Seed planter, hedonist
heathen when the unwise son fell to pieces

Purposeless when the father
flew for cover

The cloven will cleave
the water finishes itself, finishes me

Stream unreeling, you are
the end of the world, an endless horizon

It's a sham, this charnel-choice
between heaven and home

Finally free of the labyrinth
and overhead nothing but sky

Sinking

you became real to me father
when I saw you fly over me from beneath the waves

a bone-white door against the cloud-white ceiling
looking for me, flapping and furious

I watched you in the dark as you slept
knowing the edge of you only by deeper darkness

below you now in the blue-black, I am a star winking out,
thinking I may wake up warm and safe in the labyrinth

and not ever do this,
not seek for the sun

oh father my storm-dark coast,
                              nothing fills

Ghost Anchor

across the street that was once a river
one friend recovers and another hovers
a leaf reaching for the rain

the bridge across the river once a street
has never been raised
an echo wells upstream to sound

bodies evaporate and
rain themselves down

> Dear hoverer in silence
> What did I at all learn
> from my lost book

Nothing drowns

Prayer

Denuded and abandoned I recite
but what do I want

To rise again from the ocean
or be buried alive in the surge and sleep

To be a fearsome range in a single body
or to wind my unity down into depth

Missing in action, ghost-like
bobbing in the distance

Singing psalms to terrify myself
into deciding:

So long liberation

My time in the world was
only a gesture

My body a lonely
stranger

an ache
I never knew

Rapture

Here is your moment to affix me
adoring blasphemer to breathlessness

I drop myself one by one
Back away sun and find me

citizen of sound or stone
At the border of light clamoring

In cathedrals of menace every cruelty
sings back to me forty voices a whole city

Devour me down and bound
submerged just off the coast

In the battle to own yourself
whom do you fight

Endless ocean no way now back to land
Cathedral unravel the moonless night

Epiphany

sky-knife open the boat to oceanic lust
I want to snake-handle but I want to be bitten

reef, ravener, revenant
remand yourselves to the undertow

sluicing from the boat edge to the self-edge
ask the wind what next blue swell

bodies unpetal to white-gray frenzy
the oar scorpions in your hand

all of us hemmed to the hull
barnacled to the underside

rain unfurling back to sky
batten me to the source

sway me dusk-crazy when you arrive

Ocean Street

to Alice Coltrane

blue or white or very far away
every avenue a rain-stroked aisle
through the wild wind's theater

far to the barque floating in the last row
your self laddered to an avenue of sound
last streak of white-gold found

in lines along the branches or in the branches
are you a branch that tries from the bark to speak
cold roar of the ocean you cannot speak

how loud the blue-gray morning
how loud when you dissolved into sound
when you dissolved April

into the soul's endless question
what was your body but a first
uncertain answer

always awakened
awakened and left

reft the wait's blue hollow
sightless an oracle trying to tell

what recedes and what's left
a shirt left crumpled in the sand

in the mist you balance on a board
the shape of a prayerbook

racing along the surface toward the rocks
finding in the water a pounding afterlife

sound that undresses itself
prayerbook spun to unravel

answering the eroding cliffs and dunes
dear orange shafts of late morning

speaking backward
and in tongues

wet-suited supplicants balancing on boards
racing for shore

how do you find your self deeply
in the forest on the ocean floor

dear snake-haired woman who wondered
to some the book in sound you wrote was thunder

it is one thing to be lost another to be left
seeking a slogan a sloka your own body

dear country-dark houseflown homewrecker
shy in the blackness telling how

you sailed again to arrive
to found yourself in sound

dear hold me seen or sign
the unsoundable notes saying

dare to leave home
drop everything

did the universe write them
or did you

every aisle a rain-stroked avenue
breathlessly quoted a letter in space
of the sea's blue promise

each spring I lie on the surface of the sea
hoping to stand aloft

my shirt crumpled in front
of the empty-hearted tree one sleeve
pointing the way to nowhere beach

wantonly disappearing every day though
I did not believe when with your breath
you made a bridge and dreamed myself wrong

my strange and weary road
my unkempt figure my blue whisper
winter god whose center

in the moment unwilling to be warm
eternal the winter eternal the wind unmaking your will

will and whisper my anger my lantern my spaceless wick
but how my tenuous prayerboard can a supplicant balancing
on the surface know anything about depth

struggling out of the waves
moon a little red illegible
whole sky starless
in the late hour I didn't tell you
wrote into me the answer or a map to follow
boardless and battered
heaved ashore on the pulled-back day
in the effort of ache
where did I swim in from
water that wholly disappears into air or
does not disappear

speaking underwater because afraid to be heard
nothing after no one waiting for me
sky and sky the same grave gray that terrifies
turning the page of breath
where I left myself without sound
into the air I spell each spring like "swan"
noises from the next room keep you awake
god that was a noise in the night at the foot of the bed
claiming kinship or revival
transcribing the ghost-notes onto the sheets
we who each divine our self in spite of ourselves
running wildly boards under our arms back into the sea

in case of warmth the oceans will rise
strange cup to move through
after the continents came together

after you swam crazy through the storm to shore
after you asked for it
after you drove yourself relentlessly into the sea

we listen to one gust after the other
a gorgeous scale in the most ordinary range
drumming the time of the sea into a signature of leaves

twenty minutes of ecstasy
blue and after the blue, blue-white
a buoy, a sandpiper, a wholesale slaughter of blue

either way the harp's plucked chords
like the fog or the answer of water
dissolved into the shore's copious footnotes

transcribing the music onto ebbing surface
a missing word where continents rub together
disappear or dispel the notion
there is any such word worth knowing

a bridge collapsing along unquelled cadences of sound
when you whisper yourself to eternity
whose name did you whisper and into whose ear

blue my promise that divided itself
from flesh into sound
and from sound to womb
womb to thrum that sundered

the water's surface clamorous and racing away
dear unjacketed traveler evaporate
ghostlike distance was that you who entered
illegible annotations in my book on surf

in the tenth hour of the fourth month of which year
god the river that raced you on the surface to shore
every I a rain-stroked avenue
breathlessly quoting rain to the sand

lean close saint nothing
send me through it sister cup

a body slides through the water
cleanly angling for rocky shore
eternal internal zephyr

men have dashed themselves to death
to feel the racing thrill
how do you pronounce year after year "home" or "death"

the ocean avenue a bridge ready to collapse
pond evaporates to air
your breath made a bridge

impatient penitents race for the exit
lean close saint everyone
I live neither here nor there

the ocean scrambling itself to answer
sketching you in pieces everywhere
in an odd scene paddling against the current

straining for shore
you drew yourself in time a backwards sign
surfing on the breath

wishing to be not an echo of the ocean but its escalation
and when I cast myself across the surface I stopped wondering
would I float or would I drown

Adrift

Oh the diminishing racket of voices
calling my name eclipsed
by the new moon and indiscernible dark

I have somehow become the center of the universe

I wept for a year on the open water
strangling myself with banishment
sensation vanishing in the depths

the rain a faded photo from fifteen years ago

I am a forgotten bit of metropolitan trash
tied to his moment of redrawing the border
between twilight and daybreak

Forever at the edge of something that could save me

And the disastrous fear of what it would take to save me
My life in its entirety only imaginary
or perhaps the rapturous notion

I cannot be saved

The Fortieth Day

Seeing your way clear
of endless storm

A raft carries you across
the unstruck sound

You leave off the body
no one's playing

Every one looking for some thing
newer than death

The Plaint of Marah, Woman of Sodom

Sundered and sinful, caught in the rain of fire
nearly devoured, now inch by long inch turning to salt,

that's me, the blasphemer, Sodomite, unsure of what's true
making a break for the shelter ahead,

wondering if it will ever sink in,
will I ever learn what we did wrong —

Drench me well, downpour, combust me to ash.
After the first deluge they lit the first fire

so now, after the city burns, a merciful downpour,
rain hitting the roof like an angelic stranger, but

who was I before the thorn of my birth pierced me,
before the thread of my death drew me through?

After the garden there was still the world,
since the womb cracked open and water poured through,

but before fire stitched me in salt to the ground, who was I,
before I traveled through a body into a body, who was I?

If I'm rain I should pray for a vessel to hold me,
If I'm vessel I should pray for the rain to fill me.

The storm has reneged on the deal to abate
and the fire itself seems eternal —

The last prophets boarded the ark for departure,
but this time amid fire I am the water —

You are ahead of me fifty-one paces,
leaning on our daughters hoping they'll hold you —

This time I cannot follow you forward,
this time I look back to the city that's burning,

and yes in that moment, doubting believer,
I was transformed into the most precious of matter,

when the first drops hit me first I was hollowed,
as the downpour commenced I could feel myself vanish —

I became one with the ground in the night of great fire
given eternal life as a priceless pillar

slowly disappearing into the infinity of matter,
not curse nor condemnation but salt into water, an endless reward —

Promisekeeper

In the place mountains keep time as they slide into the sea
You made a promise you never kept

You fastened yourself lonely to everything that lived
Wanted to open every closed door

Wanted to turn your back on the sky
And teach yourself how to fly

Speak in the language of myth and flowers if you must
But translate it at least for the stone and dust

You built a tower to god out of bricks and mud
When you should have built it with breath

Wings will not carry you skyward
Your own body is the only mosque you need

The tongue in your mouth the only rock
From which you could ever launch yourself into heaven

3

Handwritten Notes on the Screenplay for
Bright Felon: The Movie

1
a man with medusa hair and smoke for eyes
has been cast to play you

he can never remember his lines
so plays each scene silent

2
the score for the great love scene in which you are finally touched:
a voice quietly saying your name

3
because of troubles with the union of you
the role of "Kazim" will be played by a figure of stone

because of trouble with the rights to your name
there will be no voice whispering only the years and miles of rain

Bright Felon Alternate Ending

In the convicted evening I am a victor struck loose and restless,
creeping for the unlocked window.

The family inside at the dinner table is mine.

Listening to the escape story on the radio, my mother's hand
freezes in the air halfway to her mouth; she realizes it's me they're
talking about.

Lightning by lightning the minute before thunder.

Streets as empty as a beach.

My hand on the cold glass.

Car alarm, tornado warning, catastrophe.

Who remembers the criminal son, free of the labyrinth and unsought,
unthought of.

When will the streetlamps blink out so my father can appear furtive at
the door and beckon me furiously in.

The Vineyard

to Fanny

White-gold light like wine or wistfulness
Walking up and down wanting the day to disappear
into god, the interloper, my body

Sitting in front of someone else's house
the in-between house
porch littered with insects, pollen, dust

The white paint of the post against the sky
The metal of the copper-green flagpole disappearing
Every time I look the light has changed

First yellow, then white, first bright, then mute
It's copied, my bravery — I've no right to it
How dare I praise the world,

barking like an ugly dog crazy for home

December

gray I bend down a crumpled flower
cold Saturday afternoon going for coffee

answering your questions one after the other
my lust copied down not on your body but

into my bible of bareness
its stolen breath wedged tight in your pocket

we can't go back and I can't press
myself against you in the wind so I say

"remember last winter
when I figured myself out"

Open House

Lost in the summer afternoon
The house's upper floors disappear

What is it for me to be
At the beginning of a new life

When I knew nothing
Of the old

The Mountain Comes to Mohammad

Everyone turned their back on me
No one would meet my eyes

I watched the surface of my life
Unfold its emptiness to the horizon

Mouth of the cave of revelation undiscovered
Church of the joyful mendicants off-limits

You don't want me to die unmourned
But even if the mountain finds me

What will happen
When I turn to stone —

Morning News

I left myself
dizzy in the sky

flint-thinking a foray
kith and kiln

humans are silent now
rude and unshaped

do you really have to sin
to be saved

what I was sick for
a glass we are filling

tool that binds me
between zenith and obscene

another season cut to pieces
soiled and squandered

what everyone knows
no one will say

Fragment

Never weather never the sky
threading my skin with fine silk lines

Ever the I that exists in air
exit me now what's shot through

Season of spring untold eternal
my body a single singing bowl

Blue weaver twist the spine of the world
in invisible ink I am written

Little current of river cloud sutra
god you sky thread spend me

The Wrestler

My flat breath grows flatter. Who am I now, thick in the tricks
the body plays? No matter.

The fact of this day on fire and these arms twisted
in the effort to master another

draws me in time breathless to afternoons as a boy slick
with sweat and laughter,

horizontal in a spin, one of us in control
and the other on his back and bested.

Later I would read in heaven's books
how my body was wrong, though limber and strong.

In the web of our efforts I aim to fix a position
where the other's strength ebbs and mine kicks in.

Strength splintered to pieces,
a shard in the other we each struggle to reach.

We give in turn, strip down and shift.
I reach for one limb with my right hand, grip harder to another with
   my left.

Our bodies flash their thunder and lack.
I strain for what I'm owed. I read heaven its riot act.

Dark Room

in her dark room she etches with acid the copper plates

lost like the storm which blew the door open

images of an endless field of sunflowers and the sky of war

lost plates like my shadow body, hers the sun body of mine

shadow of my sun body says: patience

sun of her shadow body says: joy

Dugout

Enslumbered trees sometimes see
the canoe inside

We disappear one from the other
sanded away

But didn't you hear the rumor
of the unencumbered current

Naked water a surgery
a navigable swoon

There is no quick way
to brightness

But the stealthy boat
yet breathes inside

Lake Animal You

dead right now
deeded soft and unmustered

who's unnameable
who's kin

cinder or tinder
ember or ash

you lose yourself
buckled to the plan

to be a body
crawling up the wet slope

hungry for hunger
so how come you at all

to words of fire
body of water

Daylight Savings

leaves orange on the ground
jealous of the trees that breathe in

both sides of life I see

the life that sees me
at the beginning of everything

who are you stranger receding

finally getting colder
my body without touching another

night gives you an hour night swipes it back

Goya's New York

I want to go home

the streets are flooded
up to the car windows

I want to drown

the loneliness of the man
in the painting about the execution

he is looking
no one else is looking

Hofmann's New York

it hardly matters my silence
weather moment or year
season gather warmth on
the surface of the sun

a body regenerates silence
button of yellow billow
red to its world paintings I
never finished suddenly

threatening to explain
a dormant tree will always
flower in my case I thought
I would be silent forever

Dry Dock

sunboat in anxious wind
frigate caught in arctic ice
bottled and wounded

ship in ice: trapped

ship in a bottle: actually built there

dry dock: a place I will never go

Monochromatic

sheets of ice on the river a soft landscape fully white
remembering when monochromatic I left him
taking the train north from winter to winter

the conductor called out each station name
we have no name for where we are now
making all local stops due to snow emergency

snowdrift: physical residue of past action
I'm like that: curled around the warm edge of his body
listening through the walls to the distorted voices of the lovers in the
       next room

I'm painting a work called "four pages from a book against war"
the last thing he said to me when I told him the train wasn't
       running express
"you'll be traveling for a really long time"

completely white vista the dimmest shift of gray against a snow dune
the soundtrack I compose for the film of this: fifty minutes of hiss
     and drone
and white noise my voice reading the work slowly without tonal shift
     or emotion

the bass groove of wheels on tracks underneath all of it
how do you hear the music of snow falling
how does the sound of snow enter your skin

Dear Shams

There's no answer to winter
sun sets over water

falling so quickly
you have not been lost

listening for silence
where and where did you go

twelve-stringed music
rejoin me

in the sun-year I swelled long shadows
in the moon-year the valley folded itself up

you are the beloved I would not love
at the fountain witless and still

a stream pours over rocks making music
could the water rush over me

could you rush
over me

the sun drops so quickly into its banishment
could I please forget to breathe and drown

will the ocean rejoin me
you have not been lost

can I be reborn as a guitar
and you reborn as music to hum inside me

one day you stopped looking at me
and I knew

the last note was lingering in the box
of my body

you did not vanish in the marketplace
I still imagine you in me as breath

broken in thirds
corded to sound

I took your name when the sun came up
sun of winter, sun windless and wistful

come down across the water
undone sun give me the drunk go-ahead

last time I searched for you
this time I stretched hollow and resonant

last time I raved without senses
this time my angel my string-singer

pluck me oh pluck
me and hum

The Argument

Waver wherever you are in the infinite world
burying yourself in stone or scripture

Thrust into a dizzy calamity of unstaked claims
you were planning to turn traitor to the sky and return home

But the letters you are written in are porous ones
that quiver fickly between liquid and vapor

Don't fake that you hate it charlatan always desperate to disappear,
to disclaim your body as a temporal site of an always unfolding soul

So here you are, tricked by eternity
suspended like an idiot between rock and wonder,

Your body screaming to sink and the hunger for bliss
dragging you out of the world yet again

You say you know what you are and what you are made of
but can you face the unending blue both above and below

I pray you unwing yourself
unwing yourself and fall

Confession

I'm drifting now cold and stolen, the sun-bound one
Giving lie to the myth I fell

Only a story spun to warn back heathen sons
Who burn too brightly

I saw the feathers flutter down like pages
From the old man's book

Dead scared of heights
I am the wrong boy for the job of proving gravity's limit

But wings are small things invented by men
Who could not but cut the cobalt sky

From the sapphire sea
But I want to weave blue and blue together

So when the feathery pages sink
Damp beneath the waves

The ink streams clear to nothing
the story goes I drowned

Dear god, father of light
I must excuse myself from the formula

Nothing adds up to me
An equation desperate to be solved

I abandoned wings and sun
For the blue direction

And by the flowers in my mouth
I swear I'll find some place on this earth that knows me

The Promise of Blue

Peak performance is meditation in motion
GREG LOUGANIS

What we wanted was to watch him silver fall
Cut the surface of the water and leave no bruise

Every earth bound angel who was taught his body was a sin
Calculates in his head equations needed to sculpt the air

As he aims from grim height for the promise of blue

Always smote by lightning, disobedient boys tumble in a tangle down
To drown in the well of others' rage or their own sorrow

Thirst to again return skyward, unbloodied and held close

But to leap is to know the body is the equation the sky has written
And around the body that launches space unfolds its shape of wings

Blue water and blue air are the same substance and within
He turns into currents and tides surging in place

Swims the endless distance down, soars sleek through the cold depth

Now years after he still sings the eerie air as he walks along
    the shore
He still knows the secret — that at every moment in the body
    and breath

One can still plummet and plunge and soar

Hymn

My father's silence I cannot brook. By now he must know I live
and well.

My heart is nickel, unearthed and sent. We are a manmade
catastrophe.

Unable to forgive, deeply mine this earthly light that swells
sickly inside.

Like wind I drift westward and profane when the doors of ice
slide open.

While he prays my father swallows the sickle moon, its bone sharp
path spent.

Preyed upon by calendars of stone unbound the nickel of the
mountain in streams.

Mine this awful empty night. Mine this unchiming bell, his
unanswered prayers.

Mine the rain-filled sandals, the road out of town. Like a wind
unbound this shining river mine —

ACKNOWLEDGMENTS

Gratitude to the following venues where some of these poems appeared
in initial forms:

American Poetry Review, Colorado Review, Denver Quarterly, Hayden's Ferry Review,
Indiana Review, Lo-Ball, Kenyon Review, National Public Radio, Poets for Living
Waters, Postcolonial Text, Third Coast, Whiskey Island.

Thanks to Marco Wilkinson, Suzanna Tamminen, April Ossmann,
Michael Dumanis, Juliet Patterson, Jeanne Marie Beaumont, Jessica Grim,
Chelsey Johnson, and Nancy Boutilier for care and attention to various
of these poems.

Thank you to Noah Hoffeld who made with me a musical version of
"Ocean Street" called "blue my promise a swan." For kind friendships in
poetry, I thank Layli Long Soldier, Rachel Tzvia Back and Stephen Motika.
For an education in spirit and body I thank Sharon Gannon, David Life,
Rima Rabbath, and Jules Febre and all teachers of Jivamukti Yoga. And to the
Community of Writers at Squaw Valley in whose space I always feel home.

Gratitudes to the Ohio Arts Council and to Oberlin College for support of
various kinds that enabled to completion of these poems.

Of course a boy must thank with all his heart his dear mother and father.

And to Lucille . . .

NOTES

Follower

    The name "Icarus" means "follower"

Journey to Providence

    "Whatever we loved has been lost . . . we are in a wilderness."
    —A Russian critic in response to Malevich's "Black Square"

    "We are all of a sudden airborne"
    a mash-up of John Yau and Agha Shahid Ali

Shrine

    made more relevant by the sheathing of Oscar Wilde's tomb

Autobiography

    epigraph from "Autobiography," The Fortieth Day, Kazim Ali (2008)

The Plaint of Marah, Woman of Sodom

    after Scott Cairns

ABOUT THE AUTHOR

KAZIM ALI is associate professor of creative writing and comparative literature at Oberlin College and teaches in the low-residency MFA program of the University of Southern Maine. He has also taught at Shippensburg University, Monroe Community College, the Culinary Institute of America, and New York University.

Ali is the author of three books of poetry, The Fortieth Day (2008), The Far Mosque (2005), and the cross-genre Bright Felon: Autobiography and Cities (2009) as well as four books of prose: the novels The Disappearance of Seth (2009) and Quinn's Passage (2005), and the essay collections Fasting for Ramadan (2011) and Orange Alert: Essays on Poetry, Art and the Architecture of Silence (2010). His poetry has been published extensively in many anthologies, including Best American Poetry 2007 and Contemporary Voices from the East: A Norton Anthology, and magazines including American Poetry Review, Best American Poetry 2007, jubilat, Barrow Street, Boston Review, and Seattle Review. He has translated works by Sohrab Sepehri, Ananda Devi, and Marguerite Duras and is the co-editor of Jean Valentine: This-World Company (2012). He is one of the founding editors of Nightboat Books.

Ali was born in the Croydon, England. He received his BA and MA from the University of Albany and an MFA from New York University. He currently resides in Oberlin, Ohio.